Contents

He Keeps Me Singing	46
(There's Within My Heart a Melody)	
Jesus Saves!	6
MY PRECIOUS FRIEND	14
He Is So Precious to Me	
I've Found a Friend	
POWER AND GLORY	11
Glory to His Name	
There Is Power in the Blood	
Sweeter as the Years Go By	24
Tell Me the Stories of Jesus	20
with Tell Me the Story of Jesus	
THE CLEANSING MEDLEY	40
At Calvary	
At the Cross	
Are You Washed in the Blood?	
THE GLADNESS MEDLEY	34
A New Name in Glory	
Since Jesus Came into My Heart	
THE GLORIFIED MARCH (Duet)	50
Nothing but the Blood	
Victory in Jesus	
When We All Get to Heaven	30

RAGS TO RICHES

Moderately Easy

Hymns and Gospel Songs à la Ragtime

Arranged for piano by
Jolene Boyd

Kansas City, MO 64141

Copyright © 1998 by Lillenas Publishing Company. All rights reserved.
Litho in U.S.A.

Mr. Garnet Six

A patriarchal saint in my church family,

who with his continued support

and growing interest in my music,

especially of rags,

has been the inspiration behind this collection.

Performance Notes

In order to translate this unique sound into hymns, it may be helpful to listen to some recording of rags before performing these arrangements. As you do, you will begin to hear signature characteristics. The left-hand march meter lays the foundation for the right hand's busy syncopation above it. Listen for certain motifs that are used repeatedly. In places, rubato is perfectly in order. Allow yourself expressive variations in tempo. You will soon hear places that cry out for a slight stretching of the tempo just before it runs away again.

Notice how often the left hand leans into the last notes of the measure with a sort of down-up effect. These I have termed "push beats." Emphasize these places, and you will instantly hear the rag sound coming to life. To keep from stiffening up, be sure to keep a loose, relaxed left hand for the rigors of the ever present back-and-forth movements. You may want to practice the left hand alone first in order to "nail those landings."

Another characteristic of rags is the dynamic contrast in the melody from soft to loud. Observe and exaggerate places where phrases are played softly first, followed by a huge sudden explosion of the sound. "He Keeps Me Singing," for instance, is a direct parody of the "The Entertainer," beginning with the introduction and on into the melody. And the ending of "Jesus Saves!" sounds like something straight out of "The Maple Leaf Rag," where it revels in the then-so-popular diminished seventh chord. You will find favored treatment of this chord elsewhere also.

Although the majority of rags are very upbeat, you will find the occasional soft, slower, reflective, and very tender rag. This is the mood I have tried to capture in "Tell Me the Stories of Jesus." And on even rarer occasions, you might find a ragtime waltz. I have included two of these in "Sweeter as the Years Go By" and "My Precious Friend."

Before you play, read the text of the hymn, and then let your fingers express the joy of your soul as you turn these rags to riches.

Jolene Boyd

Jesus Saves!

WILLIAM J. KIRKPATRICK
Arranged by Jolene Boyd

Arr. ©1998 by Lillenas Publishing Company (SESAC). All rights reserved.
Administered by The Copyright Company, 40 Music Square East, Nashville, TN 37203.

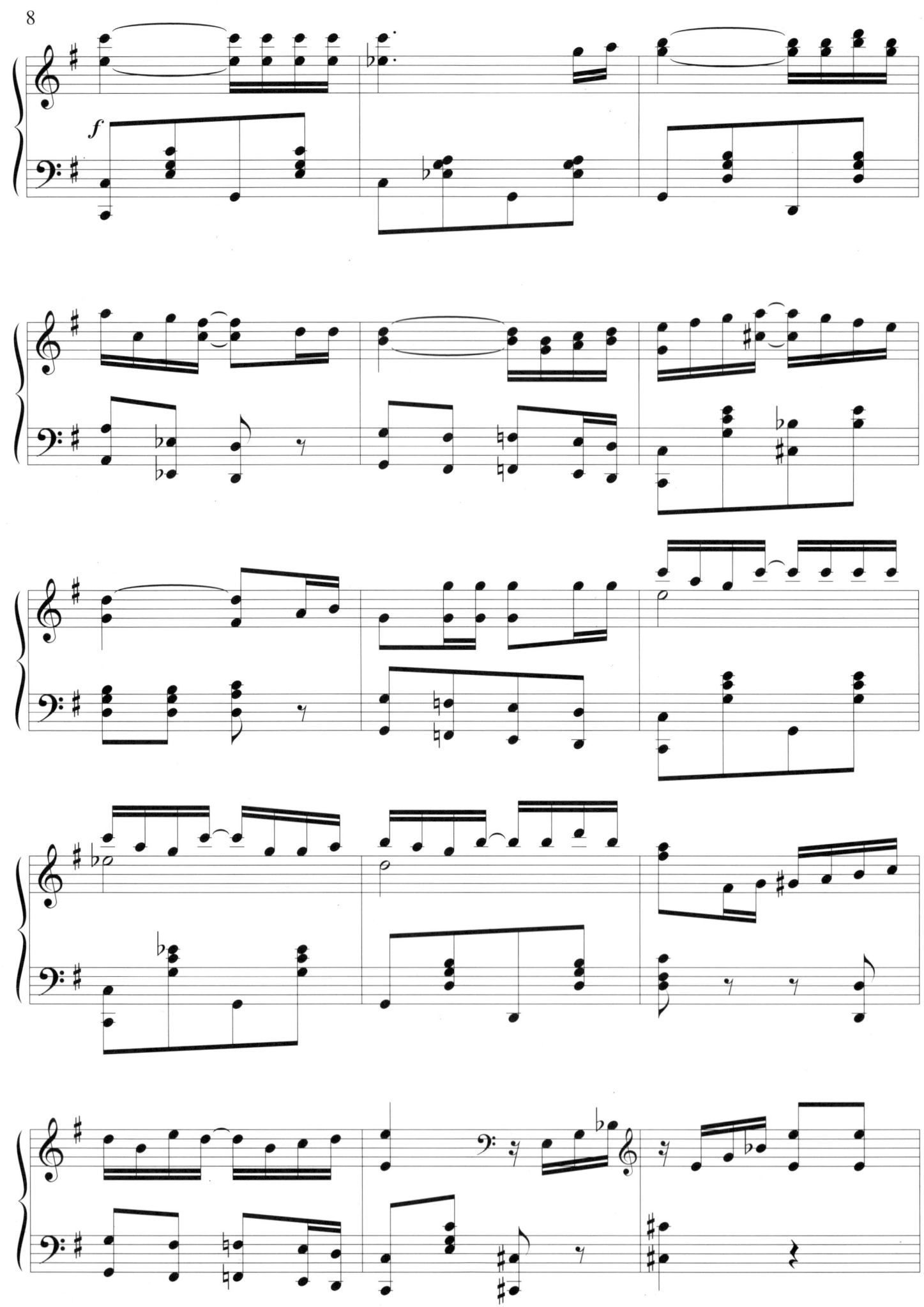

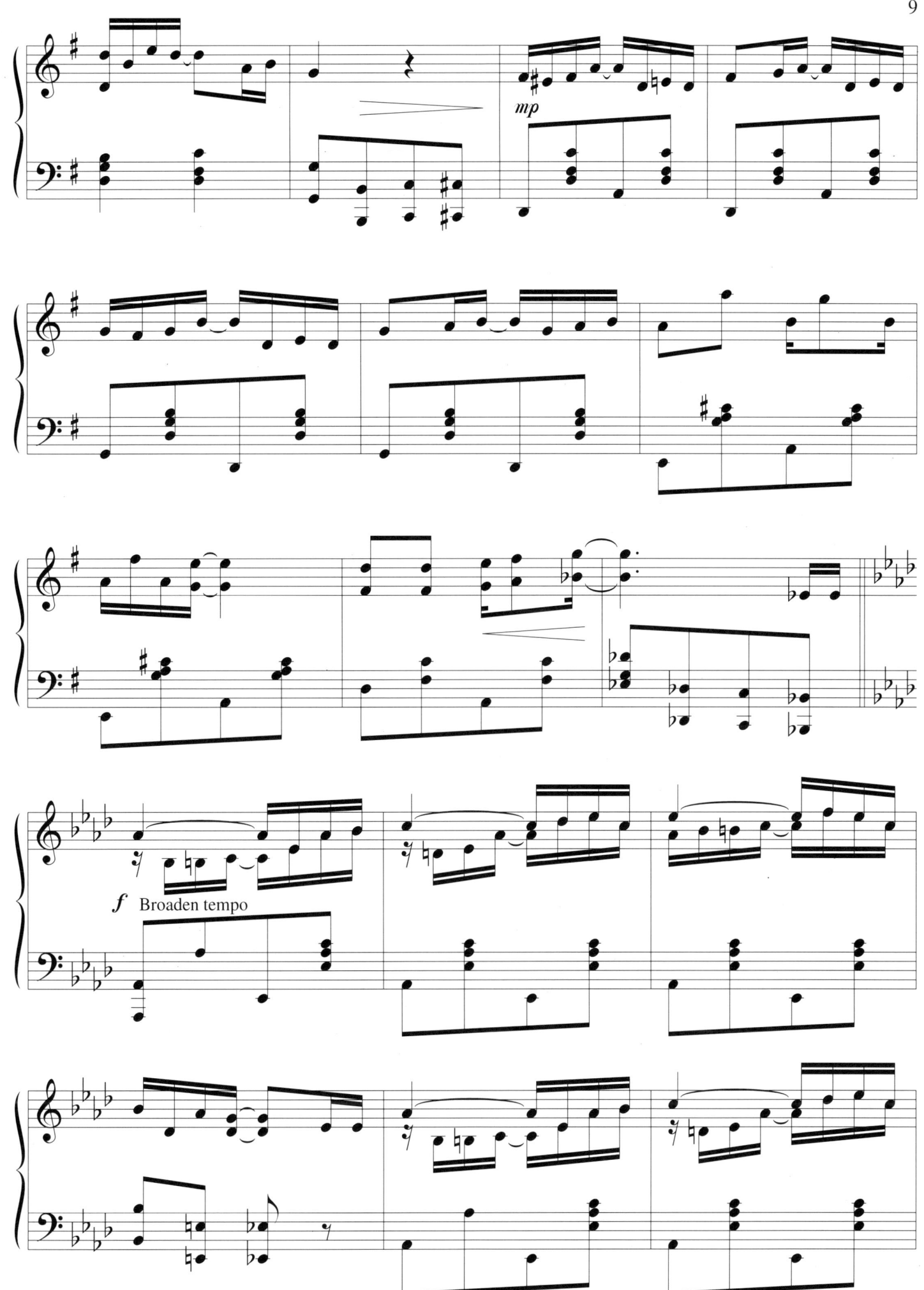

Power and Glory

Glory to His Name
There is Power in the Blood

Arranged by Jolene Boyd

"Glory to His Name" (John H. Stockton)
R.H. 8va 2nd time

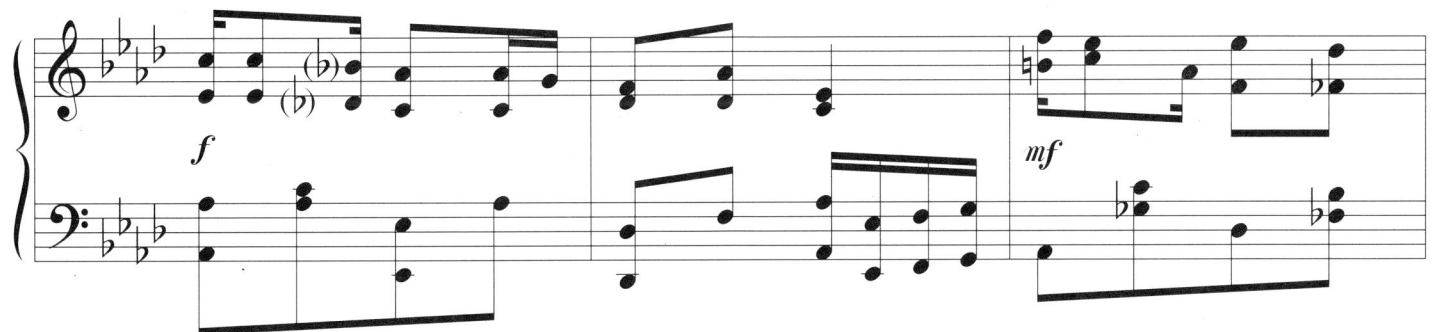

Copyright © 1998 by Lillenas Publishing Company (SESAC). All rights reserved.
Administered by The Copyright Company, 40 Music Square East, Nashville, TN 37203.

12

Bring out melody
loco both times

"There is Power in the Blood" (Lewis E. Jones)

My Precious Friend

He Is So Precious to Me
I've Found a Friend

Arranged by Jolene Boyd

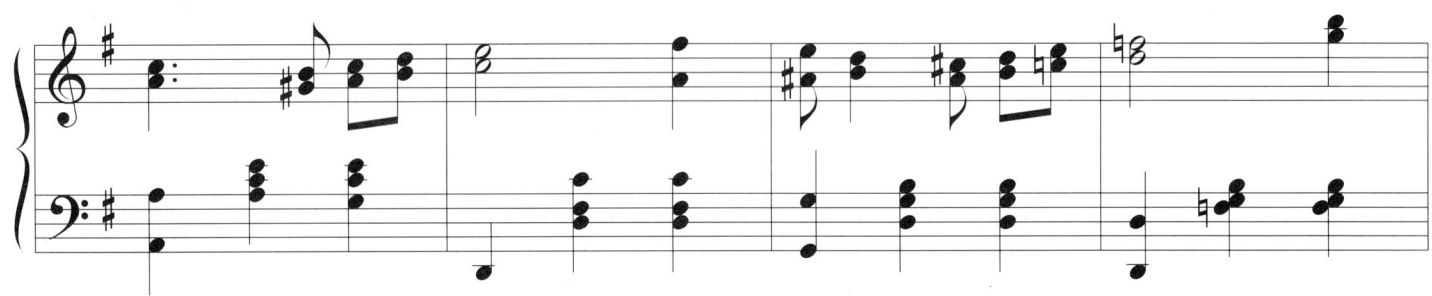

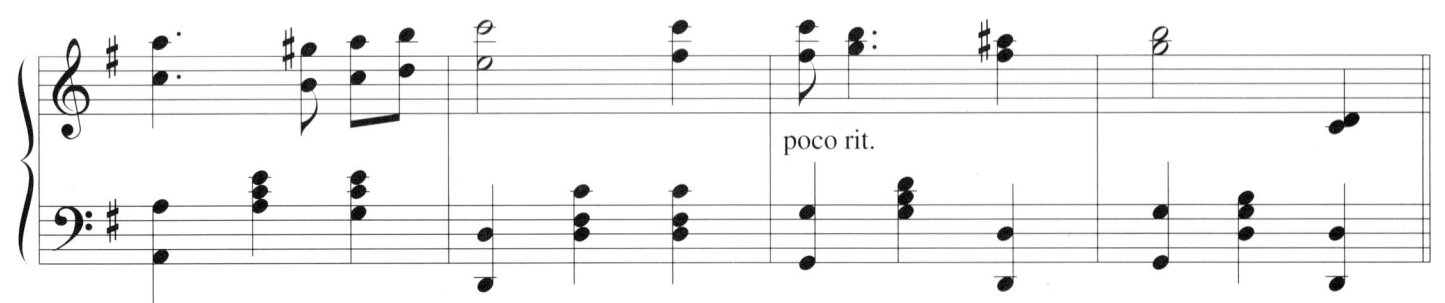

Copyright © 1998 by Lillenas Publishing Company (SESAC). All rights reserved.
Administered by The Copyright Company, 40 Music Square East, Nashville, TN 37203.

"He Is So Precious to Me" (Charles H. Gabriel)

a tempo

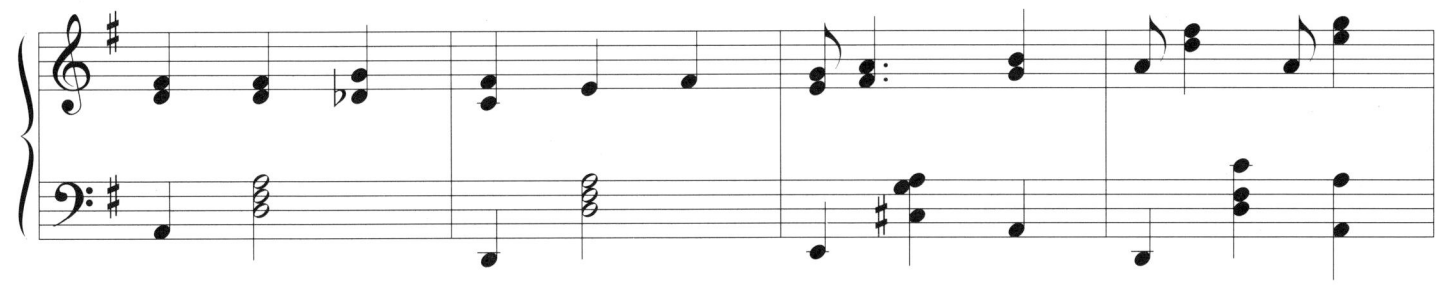

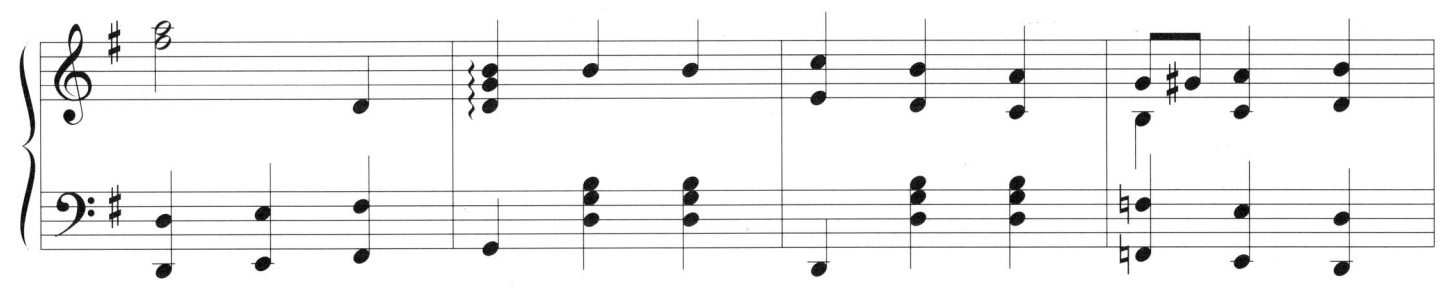

ten.

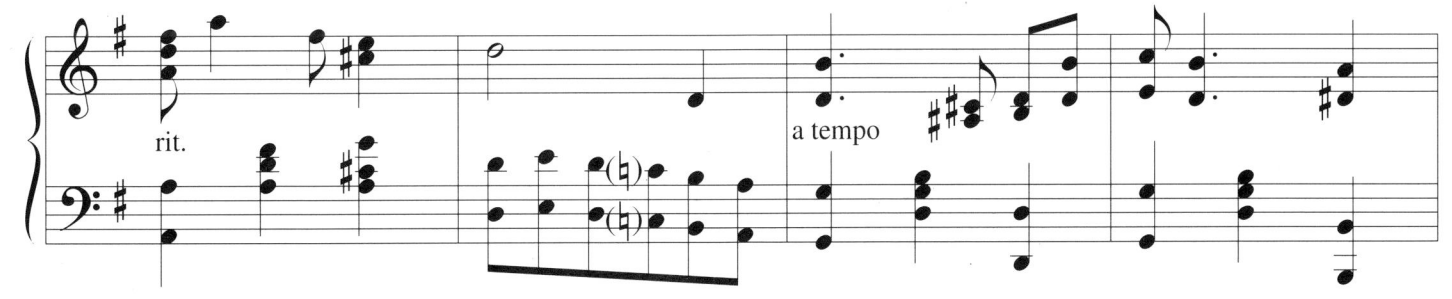

rit.   a tempo

"I've Found a Friend" (George C. Stebbins)

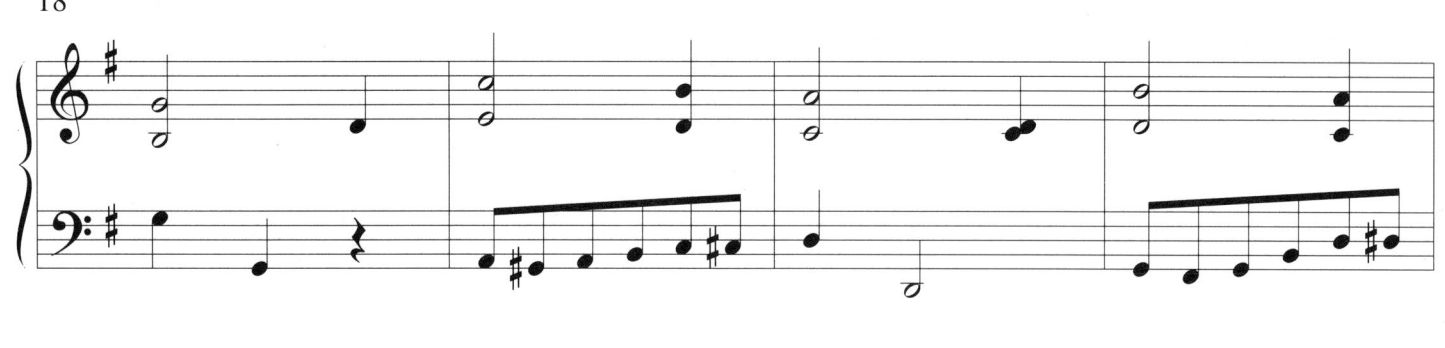
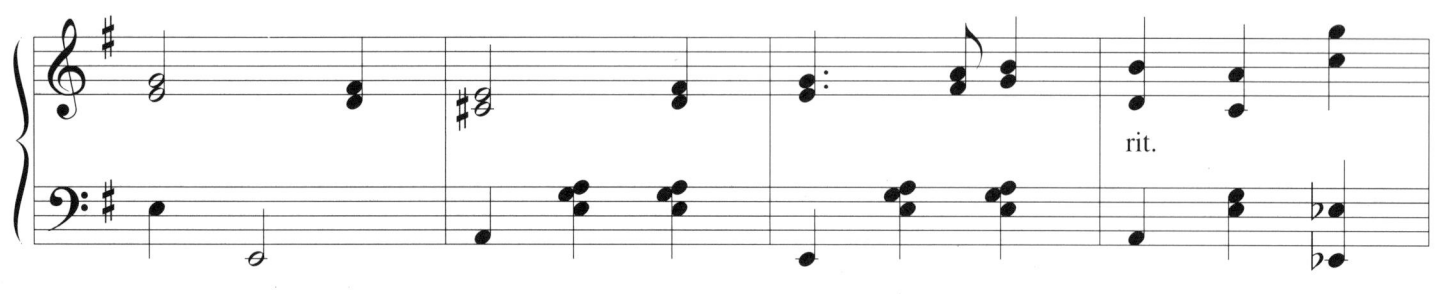

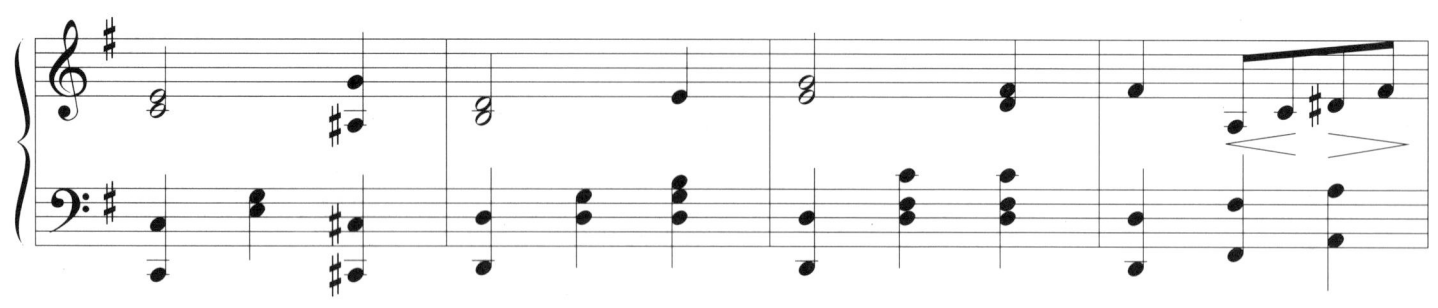

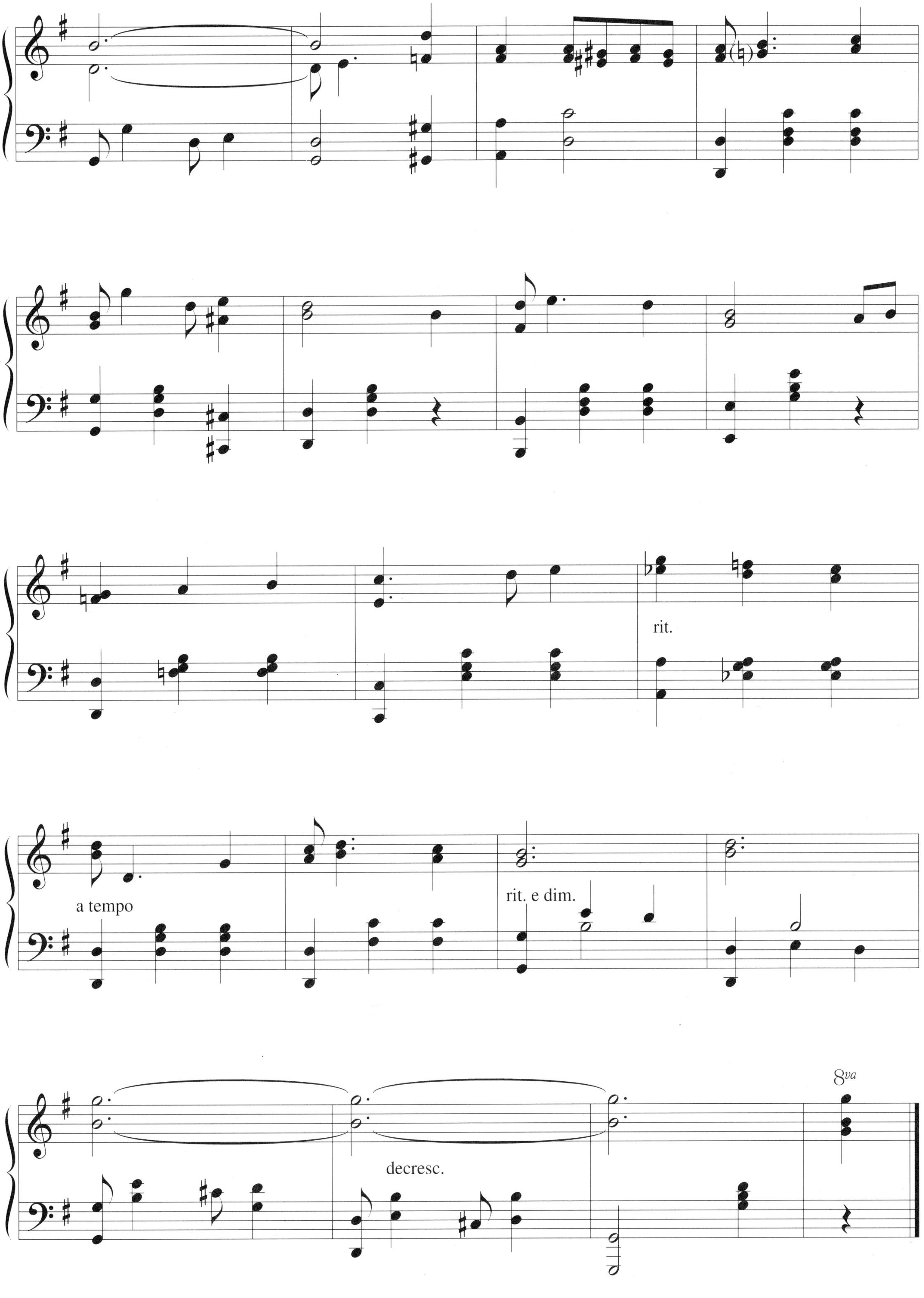
rit.
a tempo
rit. e dim.
8va
decresc.

Tell Me the Stories of Jesus

with
Tell Me the Story of Jesus

FREDERIC A. CHALLINOR
Arranged by Jolene Boyd

Arr. ©1998 by Lillenas Publishing Company (SESAC). All rights reserved.
Administered by The Copyright Company, 40 Music Square East, Nashville, TN 37203.

21

*"Tell Me the Story of Jesus" (John R. Sweeney)

*Arr. ©1998 by Lillenas Publishing Company (SESAC). All rights reserved. Administered by The Copyright Company, 40 Music Square East, Nashville, TN 37203.

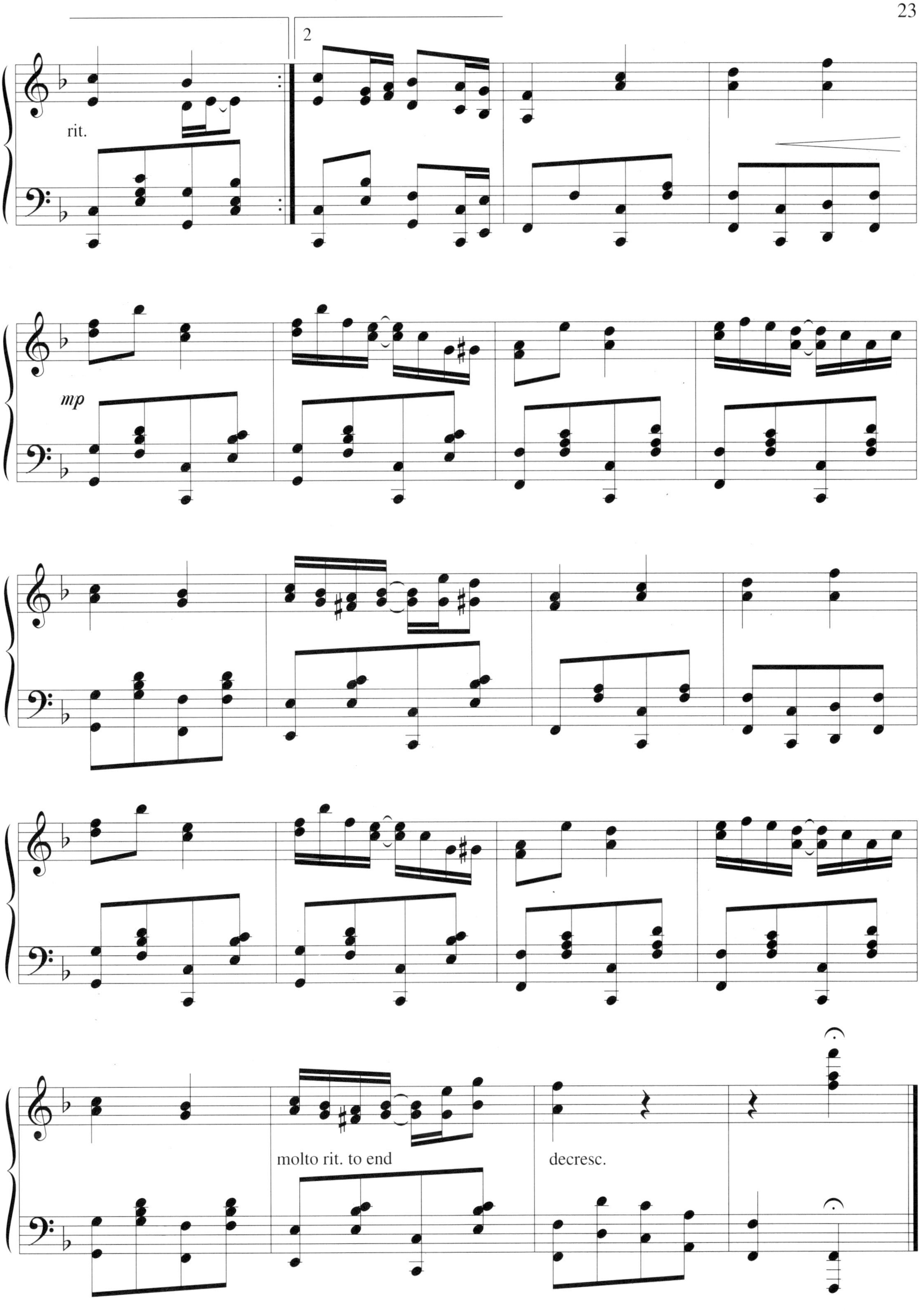
2
rit.
mp
molto rit. to end
decresc.

Sweeter as the Years Go By

LELIA N. MORRIS
Arranged by Jolene Boyd

Ragtime waltz feel ♩=ca. 100

When We All Get to Heaven

EMILY D. WILSON
Arranged by Jolene Boyd

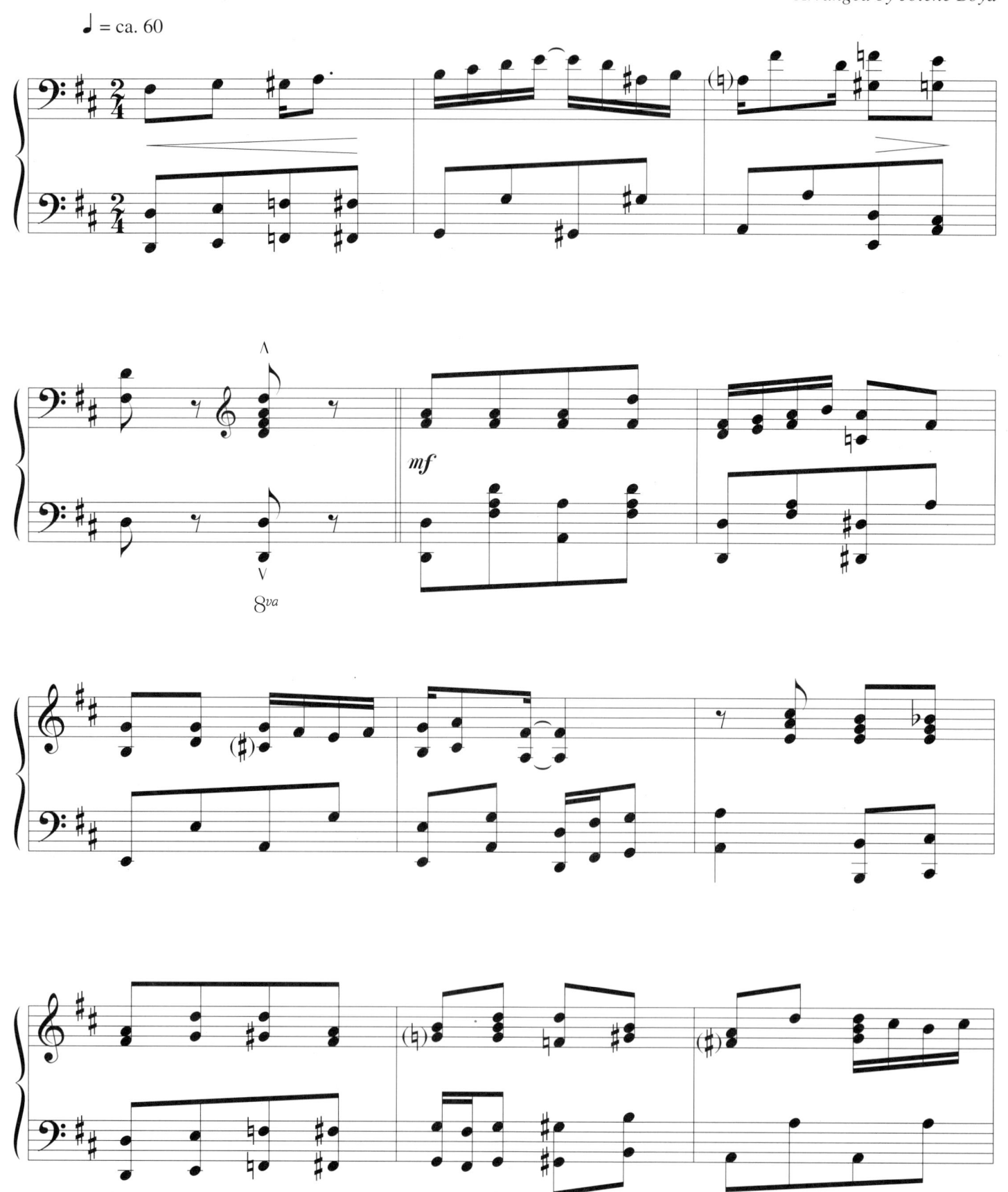

Arr. © 1998 by Lillenas Publishing Company (SESAC). All rights reserved.
Administered by The Copyright Company, 40 Music Square East, Nashville, TN 37203.

The Gladness Medley

A New Name in Glory
Since Jesus Came into My Heart

Arranged by Jolene Boyd

Copyright © 1998 by Lillenas Publishing Company (SESAC). All rights reserved.
Administered by The Copyright Company, 40 Music Square East, Nashville, TN 37203.

"A New Name in Glory" (C. Austin Miles)

36

"Since Jesus Came into My Heart" (Charles H. Gabriel)

38

39

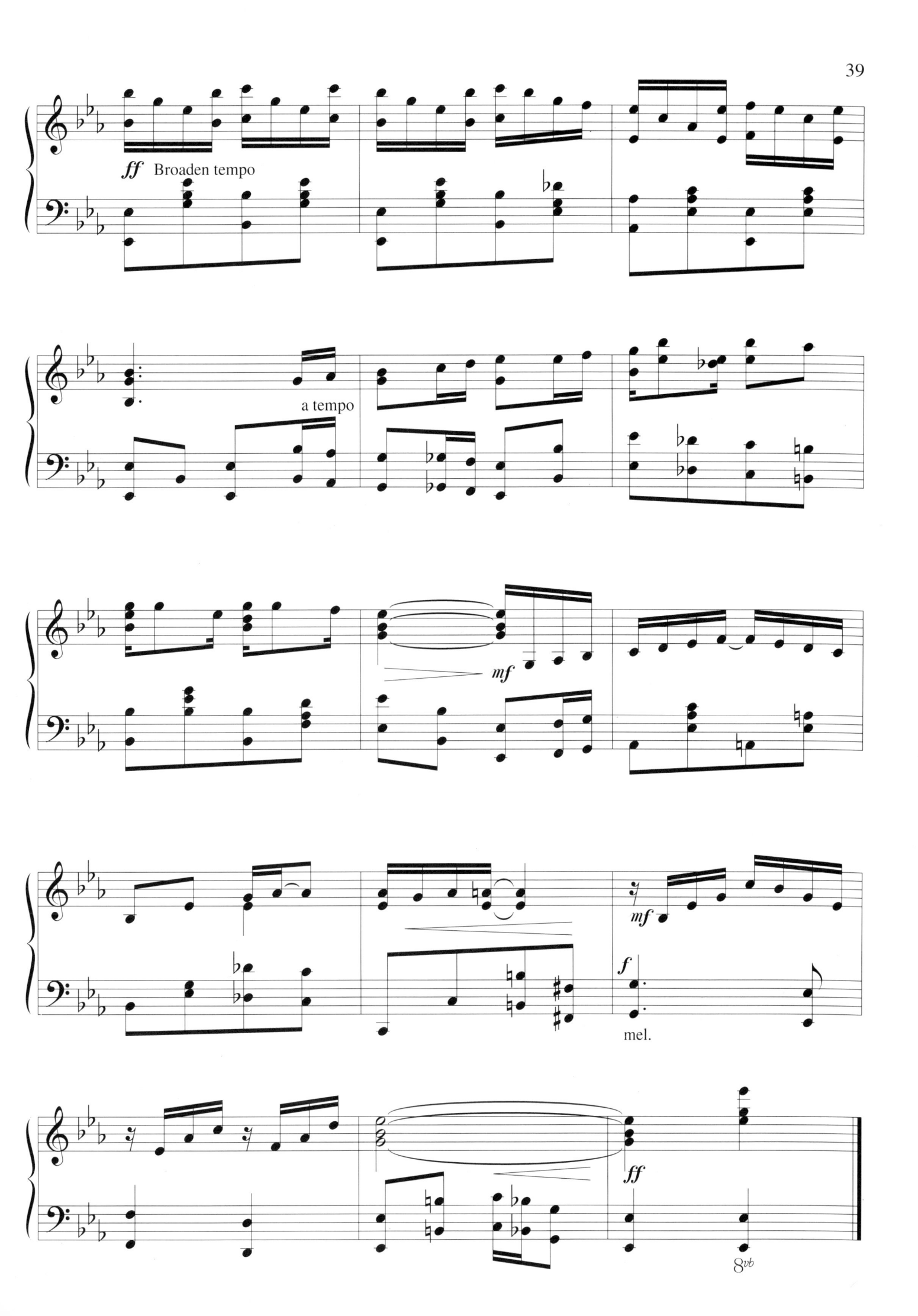

The Cleansing Medley

At Calvary
At the Cross
Are You Washed in the Blood?

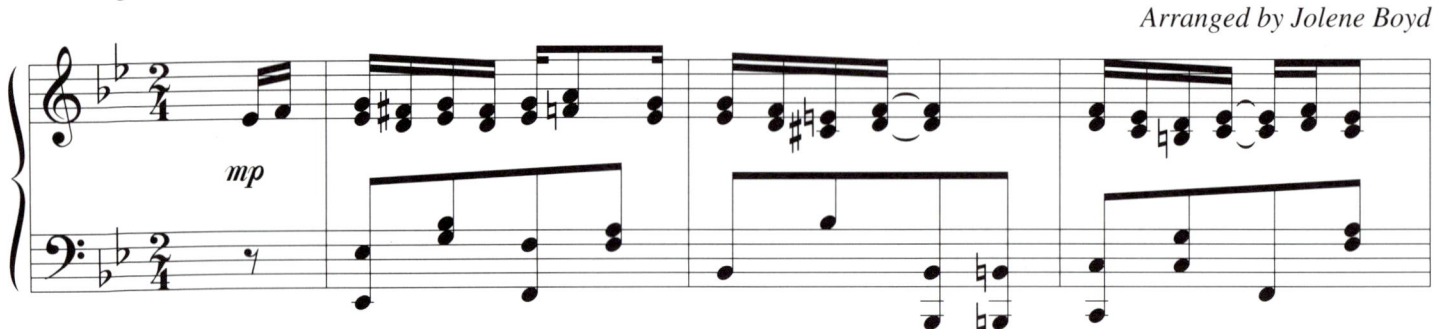

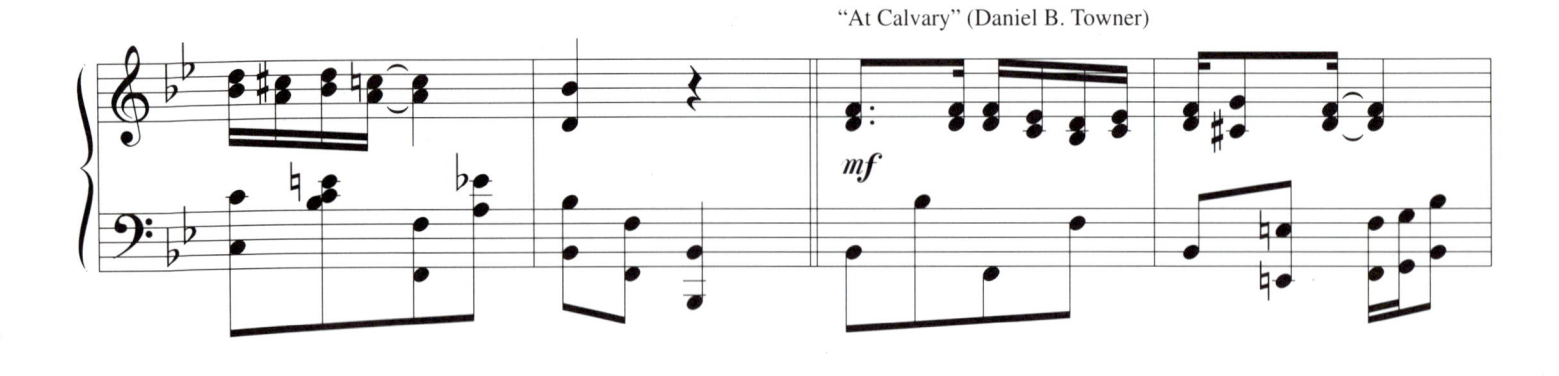

Arranged by Jolene Boyd

♩ = ca. 63

"At Calvary" (Daniel B. Towner)

Copyright © 1998 by Lillenas Publishing Company (SESAC). All rights reserved.
Administered by The Copyright Company, 40 Music Square East, Nashville, TN 37203.

41

poco rit.

a tempo

"At the Cross" (Ralph E. Hudson)

mp

f   mp

42

"Are You Washed in the Blood?" (Elisha A. Hoffman)

44

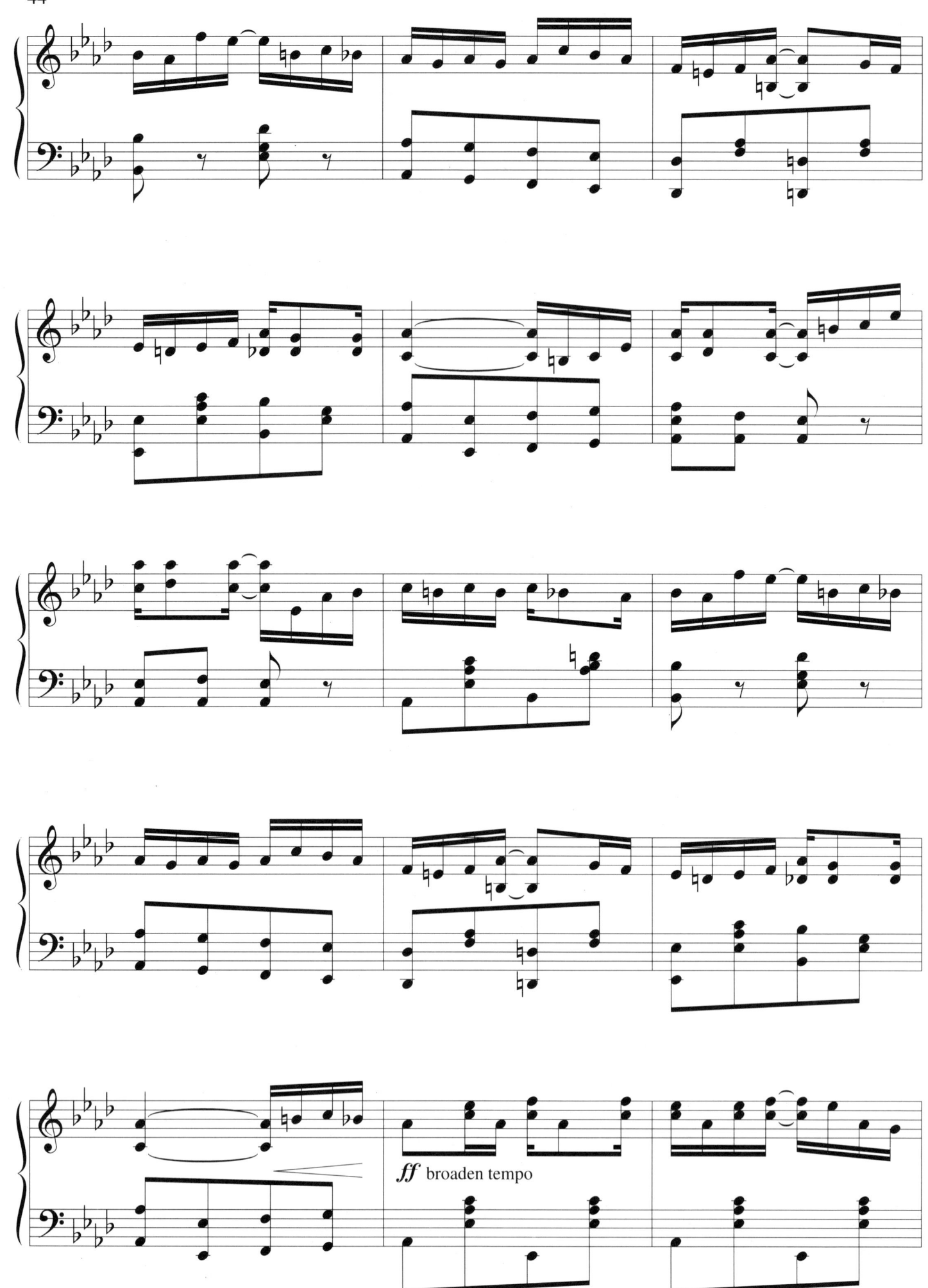

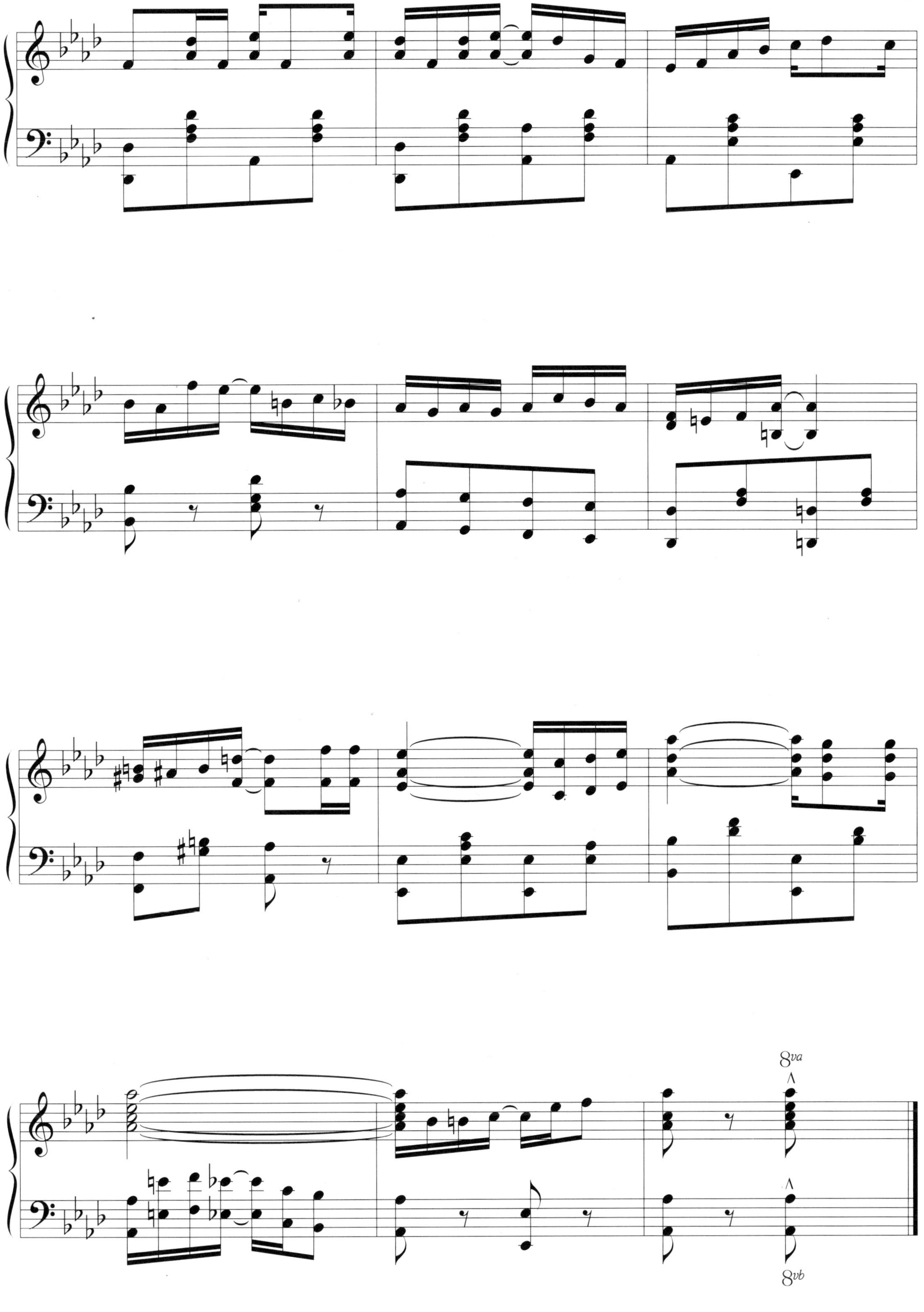
8va
8vb

He Keeps Me Singing
(There's Within My Heart a Melody)

LUTHER B. BRIDGERS
Arranged by Jolene Boyd

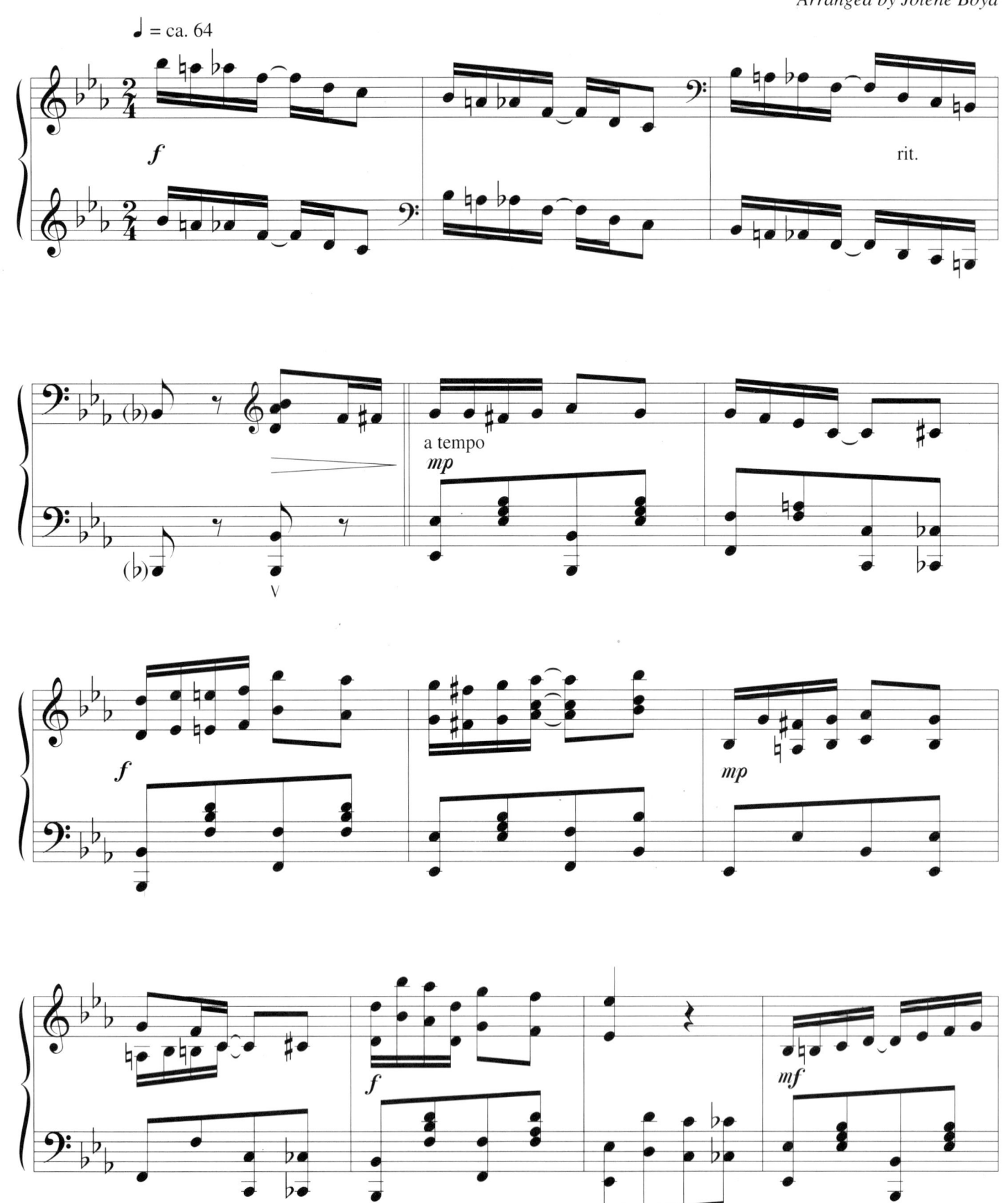

Arr. © 1998 by Lillenas Publishing Company (SESAC). All rights reserved.
Administered by The Copyright Company, 40 Music Square East, Nashville, TN 37203.

47

48

49

The Glorified March

Nothing but the Blood
Victory in Jesus
Secondary

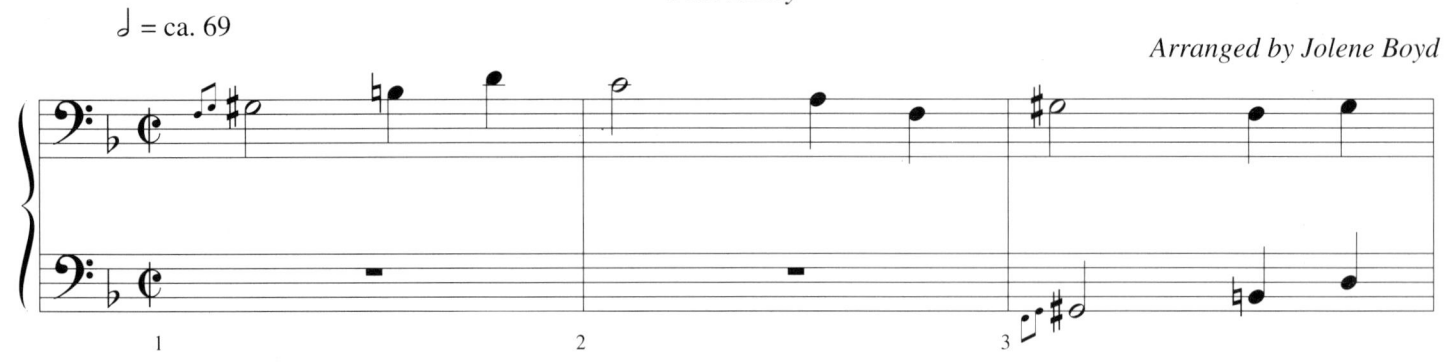

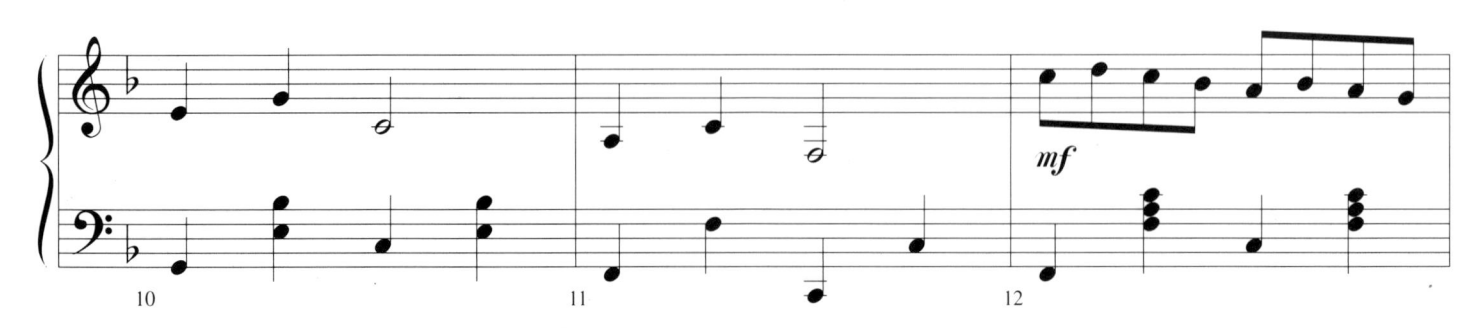

Arranged by Jolene Boyd

*"Nothing but the Blood" (Robert Lowry)

*Arr. © 1998 by Lillenas Publishing Company (SESAC). All rights reserved. Administered by The Copyright Company, 40 Music Square East, Nashville, TN 37203.

The Glorified March

Nothing but the Blood
Victory in Jesus
Primary

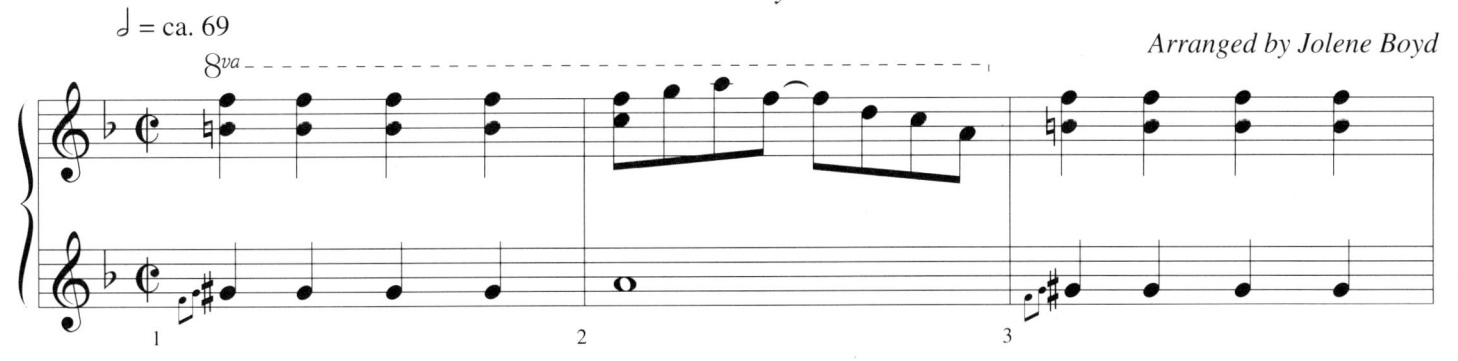

Arranged by Jolene Boyd

♩ = ca. 69

*"Nothing but the Blood" (Robert Lowry)

*Arr. © 1998 by Lillenas Publishing Company (SESAC). All rights reserved. Administered by The Copyright Company, 40 Music Square East, Nashville, TN 37203.

f
13
14
15
f
16
17
18
mf no ped.
19
20
21
mel.
resume ped.
f
22
23
24
25
26
27

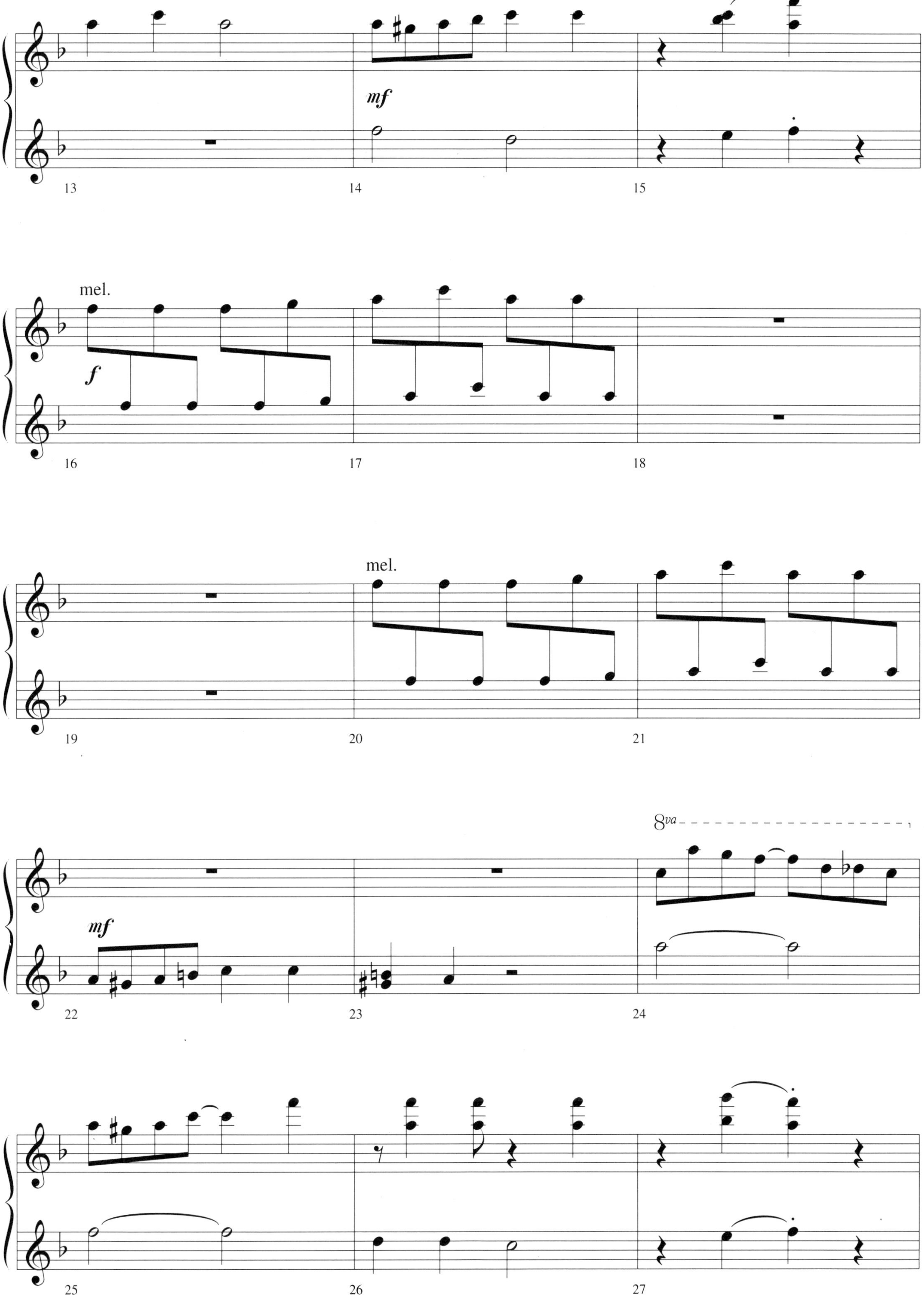
mf
mel.
f
mel.
mf
8va

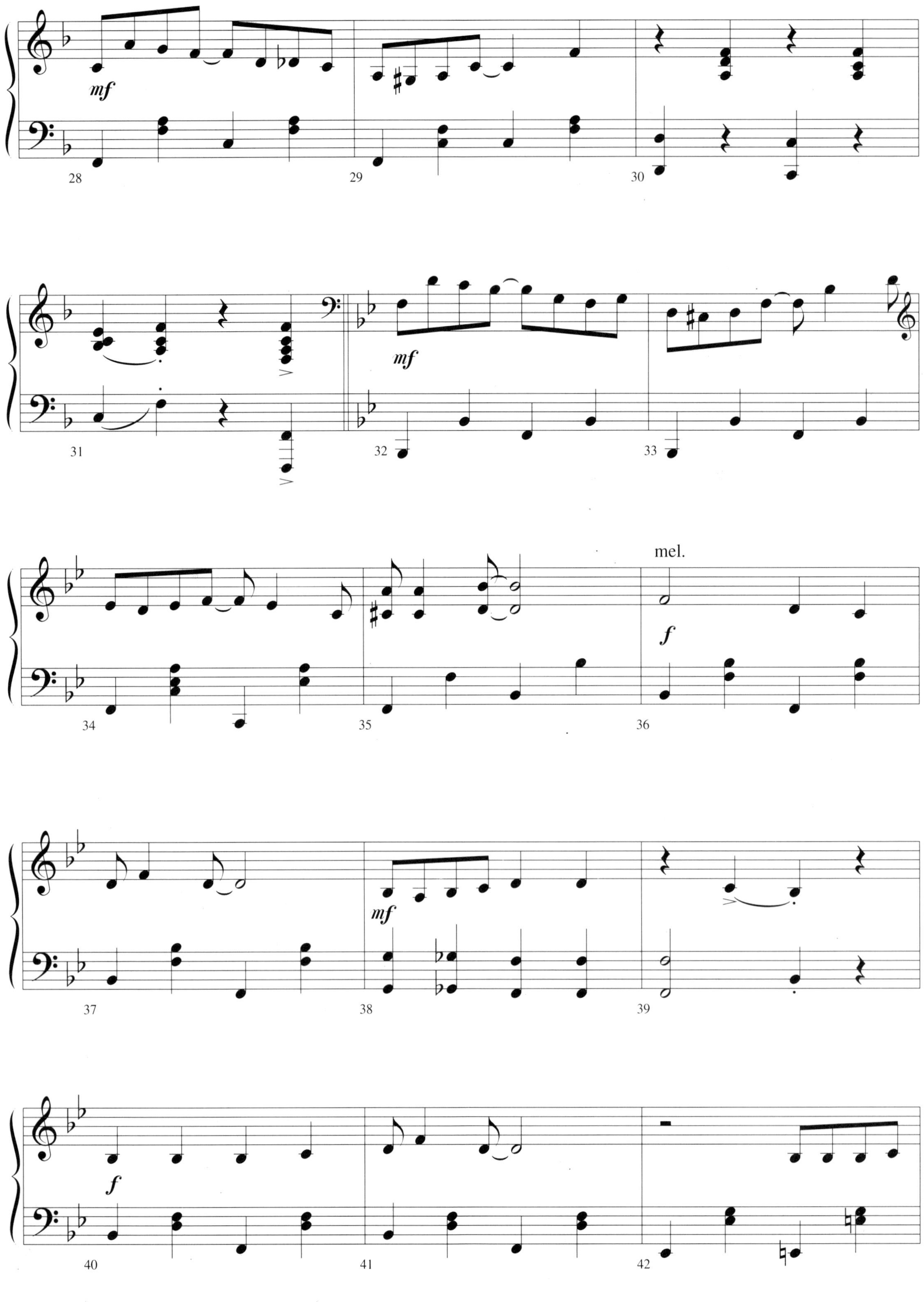
mf
mf
mel.
f
mf
f

mel.
f
28
29
30
8va
mel.
f
31
32
33
mf
34
35
36
1 2 1
mel.
f
37
38
39
1 2 1
mf
40
41
42

56

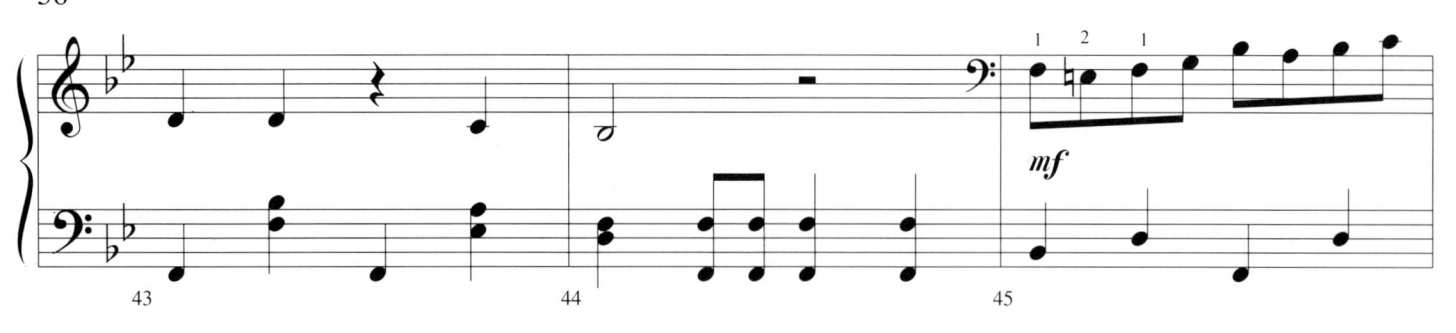

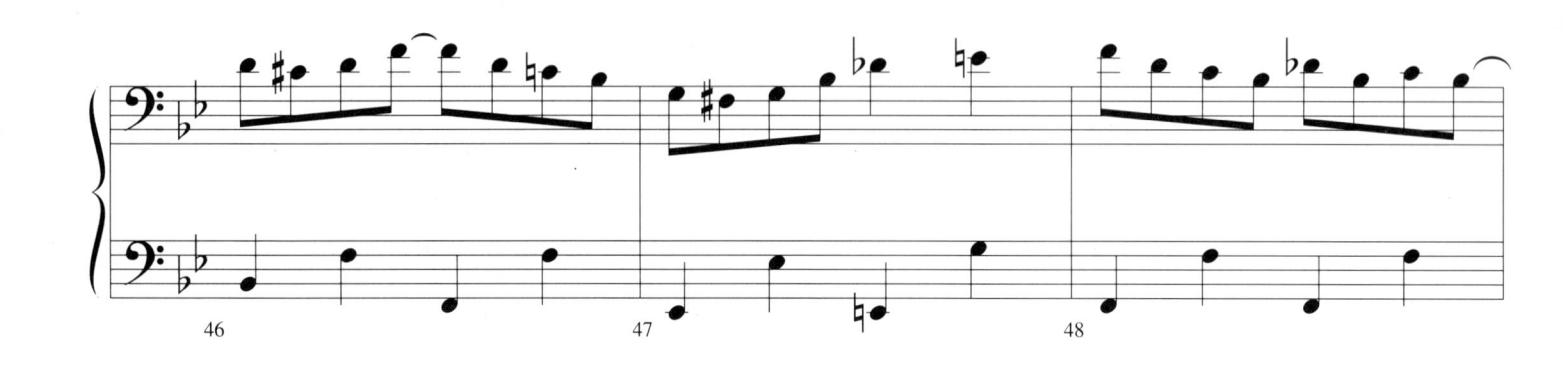

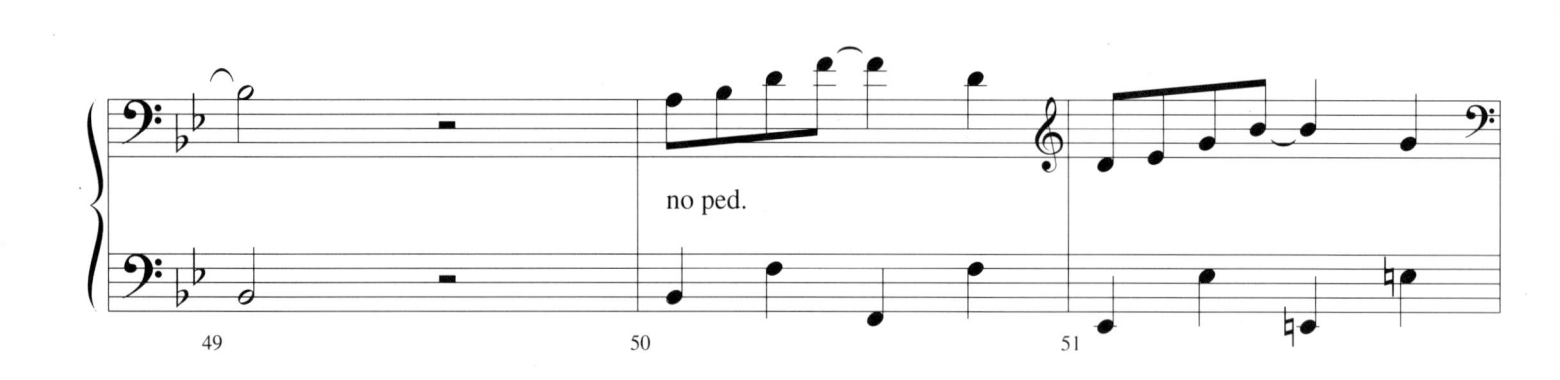

57

"Victory in Jesus" (Eugene M. Bartlett)

*© Copyright 1939 by E.M. Bartlett. Copyright 1967 by Mrs. E.M. Bartlett, renewal. Assigned to Albert E. Brumley & Sons. All rights reserved. Used by permission of Integrated Copyright Group, Inc.

59

*"Victory in Jesus" (Eugene M. Bartlett)

*© Copyright 1939 by E.M. Bartlett. Copyright 1967 by Mrs. E.M. Bartlett, renewal. Assigned to Albert E. Brumley & Sons. All rights reserved. Used by permission of Integrated Copyright Group, Inc.

60

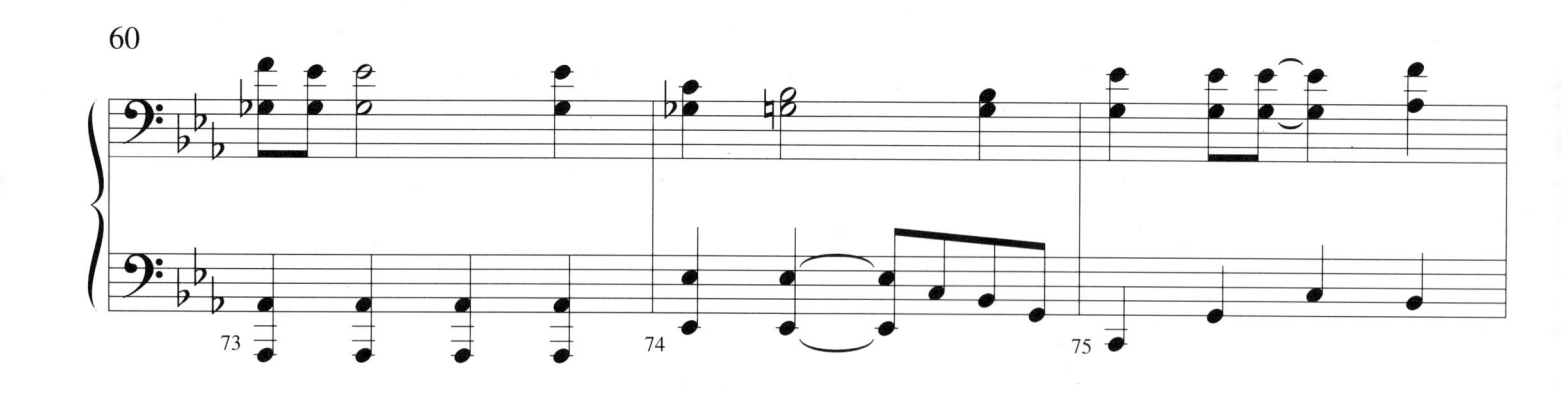

61

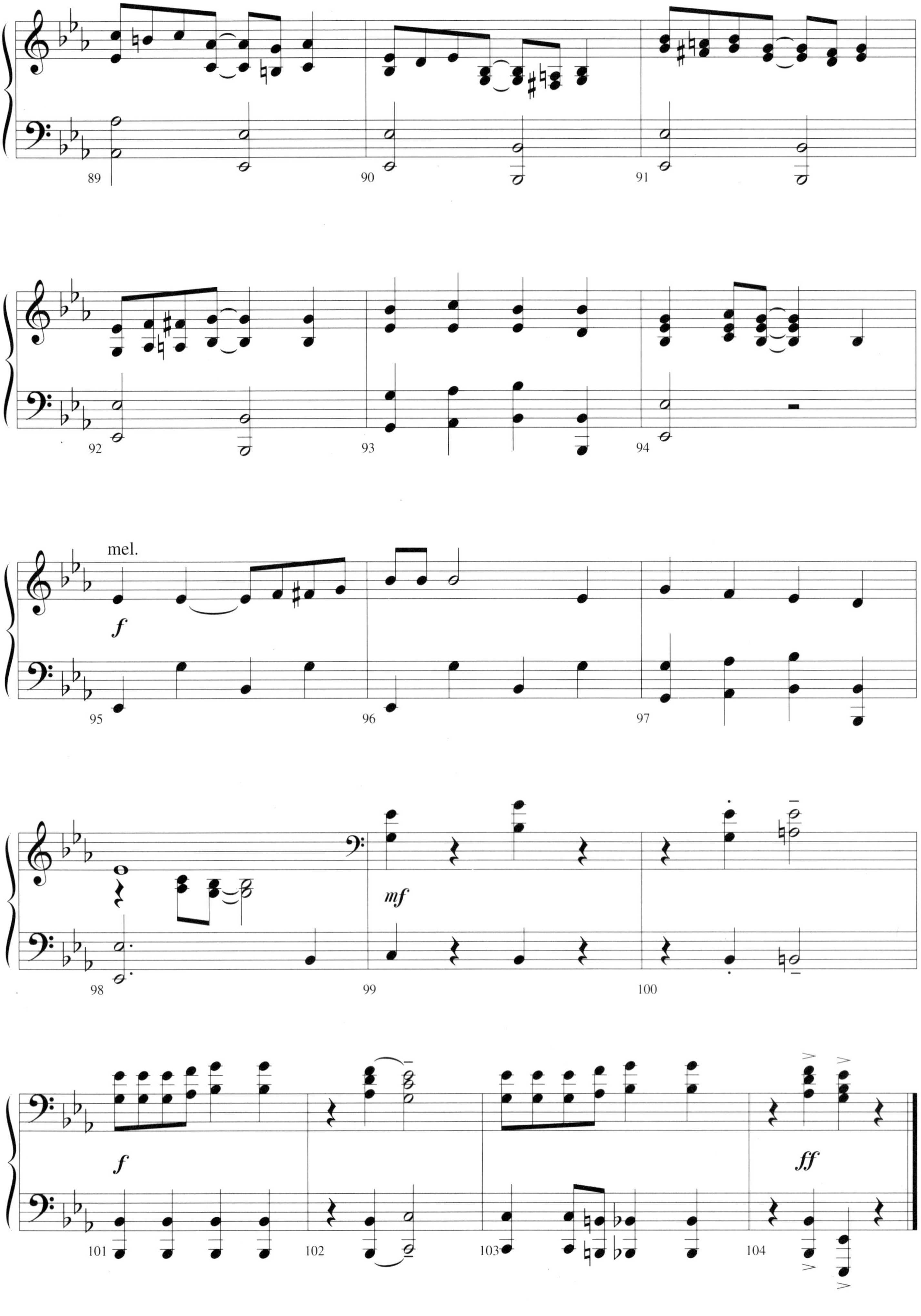
89
90
91
92
93
94
mel.
f
95
96
97
mf
98
99
100
f
ff
101
102
103
104

63